My First Book about the Alphabet of Endangered Animals

Amazing Animal Books Children's Picture Books

By Molly Davidson

Mendon Cottage Books

I0439602

JD-Biz Publishing

Read More Amazing Animal Books

Purchase at Amazon.com

Download Free Books!
http://MendonCottageBooks.com

Introduction

There are different levels on the endangered scale, including extinct, critically endangered, endangered, vulnerable, near threatened, and least concern.

Extinct animals are no longer living on the Earth, like the dinosaurs.

Critically endangered means that animal is at an *extremely high* risk for becoming extinct in the wild.

Endangered just means that an animal is at a *very high* risk for becoming extinct in the wild.

The biggest threat to most animals is humans; we are destroying and taking over their habitats.

Humans are also over killing and illegally hunting several endangered animals.

 is for an African Penguin.

African penguins are endangered, there are about 140,000 left in the wild, that is only 10% as many as 1900.

They are the only penguins that live on the coast of Africa, and the surrounding islands.

 **is for a Borneo Elephant.**

The Borneo elephant is critically endangered, and there are only between 1,000 - 1,600 left in the wild.

C is for a Chimpanzee.

Chimpanzees live in the tropical forests of
Africa, where they are endangered, with only
about 100,000 living in the wild.

D is for a Dhole.

The Dhole, as called the Indian Wild Dog, is an endangered animal with less than 2,000 living in the wild.

They live in packs in the jungles of Asia.

They can run up to 45 mph.

E is for an Eastern Gorilla.

Eastern Gorillas live in the tropical jungles of Eastern Asia, where they are endangered with less than 5,000 living in the wild.

They are the largest primates in the World, weighing about 500 pounds and standing almost 6 feet tall.

F is for a Fin Whale.

Aqqa Rosing-Asvid © <u>Wikimedia Commons</u>

The endangered fin whale can be seen swimming in all the World's oceans.

They are the second largest animal in the World, the biggest is the blue whale, it weighs 150,000 pounds and is up to 79 feet long.

G is for a Giant Panda Bear.

There are only about 1,500 endangered giant pandas left living in the mountains of China.

A giant panda will spend between 12 - 15 hours per day eating bamboo.

 **is for a Humboldt Penguin.**

Humboldt penguins are a vulnerable species living on the coast of South America, in Peru and Chile.

I is for an Iberian Lynx.

The Iberian lynx is a critically endangered animal that live on the Iberian Peninsula in southwest Europe.

There were about 3,000 lynx in 1960, now there are less than 300 living in the wild.

J

is for a Javan Rhinoceros.

The few critically endangered Javan Rhinos
live in the rainforests of Southeast Asia.

 **is for a Killer Whale.**

The endangered killer whale, also called an orca, live in all the World's oceans.

They are killed for their meat and blubber, which is used by some for fuel.

They swim about 26 mph and can swim for over 50 miles without stopping.

L is for a Leatherback Turtle.

The critically endangered leatherback turtle swims in the Atlantic and Pacific Oceans.

Sea turtles have swam in the oceans for over 100 million years.

M is for a Macaw.

The endangered macaw lives in flocks of up to 30 birds, in the tropical forests of Central and South America.

 is for a Numbat.

There are about 1,500 endangered numbats living in Western Australia.

Numbats are a marsupial, but they do not have a pouch on their belly and they eat termites and ants.

O

is for an Orangutan.

Orangutans that live in the forests of Asia are critically endangered.

Orangutan means "man of the forest" in the Malay language; they help spread seeds around the jungle floor helping more plants to grow.

P is for a Pygmy Hippopotamus.

The endangered pygmy hippo lives in the swamps and forests of West Africa.

They weigh about 600 pounds, which is about 1/5 the size of a regular hippo.

P is also for a Pangolin.

The critically endangered pangolin lives in forests and grasslands in Asia and Africa.

The word pangolin, in the Malay language, means roller, since a pangolin will curl up and roll into a ball if threatened.

 **is for a Quokka.**

The vulnerable quokka is the World's smallest wallaby, which is found living in south -west Australia.

 is for a Red Panda.

![Red panda climbing on a wooden branch]

The endangered red panda lives in the mountains of the Himalayas.

Only about 20% of red pandas survive until adulthood.

S is for a Sea Lion.

Endangered sea lions swim in all the oceans, except the Atlantic.

They like to gather in large groups on rocky ocean harbors, where they can take a break and soak up the sun.

S is also for a Saola.

Silviculture © <u>Wikimedia Commons</u>

Critically endangered Saolas only live in the Annamite Mountains of Vietnam and Laos.

T is for a Tarsier.

The endangered tarsier monkey lives in the forests of south-east Asia.

They can jump 40 times as long as its body length.

U is for an Umbrellabird.

Francesco Veronesi © <u>Wikimedia Commons</u>

The vulnerable umbrellabird lives in the rainforests of Central and South America.

V is for a Vaquita.

Paula Olson, NOAA © Wikimedia Commons

Vaquita are a critically endangered porpoise that lives only Mexico's Gulf of California.

These rare dolphins weren't discovered until 1958, and now there are less than 100 left.

They will likely become extinct by 2018, if gillnets are not fully banned.

 **is for a White Tiger.**

The critically endangered white tiger lives in jungles in India, but most are being protected in sanctuaries and zoos around the World.

They are a large tiger weigh up to 660 pounds and measuring 11 feet long.

 **is for a Yellow-Eyed Penguin.**

The endangered yellow-eyed penguin lives on the sandy coast of New Zealand.

They have a bright yellow band around their eyes and pink feet.

Conclusion

I hope you have learned about many amazing endangered animals.

If you would like to help endangered animals, look online for conservation groups in your area.

Our books are available at

1. Amazon.com

2. Barnes and Noble

3. Itunes

4. Kobo

5. Smashwords

6. Google Play Books

Download Free Books!
http://MendonCottageBooks.com

Publisher

JD-Biz Corp

P O Box 374

Mendon, Utah 84325

http://www.jd-biz.com/

www.ingramcontent.com/pod-product-compliance
Lightning Source LLC
Chambersburg PA
CBHW050857290526
45792CB00002B/625